fulfilling the dream

A STORY OF HOW BOB WELKER EXERCISED HIS GIFTS TO FOUND WELKER ENGINEERING

BOB CRAIG

Fulfilling the Dream

A Story of How Bob Welker Exercised His Gifts to Found Welker Engineering

ISBN-10: 1-9398-15-48-7
ISBN-13: 978-1-939815-48-4
eISBN-10: 1-939815-51-7
eISBN-13: 978-1-939815-51-4

Table of Contents

A Word

I was introduced to Bob and Shirley Welker at one of their annual fish fries at their Star Ranch. It was 1993, and the fish was served in the hallway of the barn built for Shirley's horses (it was not your usual barn). Bob graciously opened his heart and hospitality to me. It was the beginning of a friendship that has lasted to this day.

Over the intervening years, I made many trips to Star Ranch to get firewood. Our children and grandchildren were always welcome at the Welkers'.

Failing health affected both our wives. My sweet Catherine had to be cared for in a nursing home. Dementia was taking her life gradually. Shirley had a stroke that concluded her mortal life. Star Ranch was on the way back home from the nursing home where I visited Catherine. I began stopping by every Wednesday for coffee and support (me for him, him for me). During one of these visits, Bob said how he wished the story of how Welker Engineering came about would be told.

We purchased a cassette recorder and began talking about his early life and the events that led to the development of Welker Engineering. This book came out of those conversations.

Bob Craig

Preface

In the Bible, Jesus tells a story in Matthew 25:14–30 that illustrates how each person is gifted with certain abilities and potential—called talents. Life presents the opportunity to do what can be done with those gifts. Some people recognize the quality of their gifts and work faithfully to maximize them. Other people, Jesus explains, do not see the value of their gifts and neglect to do anything with them. They blame God for not giving them more.

Jesus's story emphasizes that there is an accounting for what a person does with what he or she has been given. Some people use their talents in a way that honors God; some do not. People who work at developing their gifts realize a gain.

Robert "Bob" Howard Welker recognized that he was gifted. Born into a family that instilled in him the virtues of hard work and benefited by grandparents who demonstrated confident—even innovative—efforts, Bob embraced the challenges of those gifts to develop a life of extraordinary testimony.

As you read, you will learn how a fertile mind, coupled with a strong work ethic and attention to God's timing, led Bob to establish a company—Welker Engineering—and be granted more than 40 patents, exemplifying for us a full, long, and honorable life.

A man's life consisteth not in the abundance of the things which he possesseth.

—Luke 12:15

The Beginning

The story begins in Van Alstyne, Texas, a town situated near the railroad stop of the Houston and Texas Central Railway. The town was established in 1872 and named after either William A. van Alstyne, a civil engineer for the railroad, or for Marie van Alstyne, a stockholder in the railroad.

Van Alstyne borders Collin and Grayson Counties in Northeast Texas. It is approximately 27 miles south of Denison, Texas, and some 50 miles north of the center of Dallas. The town was incorporated in 1890 with a population of about 400 souls. Most of the economy was related to agriculture. Van Alstyne was where Louis Welker had his leather shop.

Louis Welker, Bob's paternal grandfather, worked in harnesses and buggies. His buggies were classic and desired by those who could afford classic buggies. His skill extended beyond making and repairing harnesses and selling buggies. He was also a champion checker master. In that leather shop were four tables where vigorous—and occasionally heated—games were played. Four loving cups were on display denoting Louis Welker as Champion Checker Player of Texas.

Charles Durning, Bob's maternal grandfather, had a 150-acre farm in the country outside Van Alstyne. He was an exceptional farmer. It was a time before much modern mechanization, and most farmers were thought to be ambitious if they were able to handle a 50-acre farm. Durning's farm was 150 acres and close to self-sufficient. All the food his family consumed was either raised (animals) or grown (vegetables). Mrs. Durning's garden was larger than an acre. She canned and preserved all they needed for an entire year.

Bob's grandfather Louis Welker (checker champion of Texas) holding Harold Jr.

Charles Durning, Flara's father. His work ethic and innovation had an inspiring influence on young Bob.

Durning's farm produced the standard crops for that area, including cotton, corn, oats, hay, and so forth. Livestock included cows, pigs, horses, mules, chickens, ducks, and turkeys. There was no electricity on the farm. Water was either drawn from the well or pumped by hand.

Charles Durning was an exceptional farmer. Everything—or anything—that needed fixing, he fixed. He butchered his own meat. He led neighboring farmers to team up to tackle common routine chores such as planting, harvesting, and baling. What would take a farmer weeks and strenuous labor to get done alone could be quickly accomplished faster and easier because of Durning's skill and leadership.

Mr. and Mrs. Louis Welker had a son named Harold who was born July 12, 1900. His ancestors hailed from Germany and Scotland. Harold worked in his father's leather shop during his school years. After graduating from high school, he went to Georgia Tech and earned a degree in civil engineering. Harold never worked a single day as a civil engineer. When he graduated in 1922, nearly all the jobs in civil engineering were on the Mississippi River. Harold had no interest in such work. There would be other options available to him.

Mr. and Mrs. Durning, Bob's maternal grandparents, had a daughter named Flara, a twin, born on March 28, 1900. Flara's ancestors came from Ireland. Flara and Floy, her twin sister, attended Mary Hardin-Baylor for a year. Flara had hoped to complete her education there, but when Floy became very ill, Flara dropped out of school to help nurse her twin back to health. Flara was never able to get back to school but did have enough education to qualify her to teach elementary school.

Harold and Flara met in high school, courted, and were married in Van Alstyne as soon as Harold graduated from Georgia Tech. Harold Eugene Welker and Flara Belle (Durning) Welker were the parents of Robert Howard Welker.

Harold became the cook for Durning's cooperative groups of farmers as they followed the harvest from farm to farm. Harold was with the teams, cooking for them as they rotated from one farm to another.

In 1924, Harold was offered a job as a math teacher and football coach in Brownwood, Texas. There were few, if any, full-time football coaches in those days. Most coaches also taught a class, often math. Flara kept the house. Harold Jr. was born while they were working and living in Brownwood.

Harold and Flara Welker, parents of Harold Jr., Charles, Nancy, Bob, and Tom

Bob, Nancy, Charles, and Tom in 1943. Note Charles's Navy gear.

Graduation program from 1922. H. E. Welker is listed as graduating from the School of Civil Engineering.

Harold with eight-month-old Robert Howard Welker

Grandmother Welker

The next year, 1925, Harold, Flara, and Harold Jr. moved to Honey Grove, Texas.

Honey Grove was discovered by Davy Crockett in 1836. Crockett was on his way to join the Texas army at San Antonio and stopped there to camp. In his correspondence to people back in Tennessee, he described it as a place of honey-filled trees. It was named Honey Grove in 1837. Samuel Erwin was the first settler of the town. His friend B. S. Walcott planned the landscaping and sold lots for building.

In Honey Grove, there is a large marker with this message:

Virginia-born Samuel Erwin was married in 1819 in Tennessee to Sally Rodgers Crisp (1795-1860), in a ceremony performed by local magistrate David Crockett. First settler in the Honey Grove area, Erwin arrived here in 1837 and surveyed land grants for other pioneers. A surveyor by profession, he platted the townsite for his friend B. S. Walcott in 1848. He was the town's first postmaster and one of Fannin County's earliest justices of the peace.

Honey Grove, dubbed the "Sweetest Town in Texas," is in Fannin County, 16 miles east of Bonham (the county seat of Fannin County), 39 miles north of Greenville, 42 miles east of Sherman, and 90 miles northeast of Dallas. Highways 82 and 56 run through the town. Many of the buildings on the town square are constructed of stone taken from the Floyd Quarry. The story of the Walcott family in Honey Grove is told in the best seller *A Woman of Independent Means.*

In the late 1800s, the Texas and Pacific Railway came through Honey Grove, resulting in a retail and shipping center for the local farmers. When Harold, Flara, and Harold Jr. moved there, the population was close to 2,600, and there were 70 or so businesses. Harold taught math and coached football. Their second son, Charles, was born in 1925 while they were in Honey Grove. Robert Howard Welker was born there on March 31, 1927. He was named after the famous golfer Bobby Jones. On Bob's birthday some years later, Shirley gave him a card that read, "1927 was a special year." Included in that card was a list of several significant happenings:

- The British Cabinet comes out in favor of voting rights for women over 21.
- Massachusetts becomes the first state to require auto insurance.
- Pan American Airways is incorporated in New York.
- Charles Lindbergh flies Atlantic alone aboard the *Spirit of St. Louis*.
- The new Ford Model A is introduced, reaches a speed of 71 mph.

These events were listed for sports:

- Johnny Weissmuller, the swimming star, sets three world records in the Olympics for swimming.
- Babe Ruth hits 60th home run of the season.
- In New York, the Yankees take the World Series in four straight over Pirates.

This was the list for arts and entertainment:

- Clara Bow stars in *It*.
- Laurel and Hardy debut.
- Music: "Ol' Man River" from *Show Boat*.
- Film: DeMille's *The King of Kings*.
- Al Jolson's *The Jazz Singer* opens.
- Duke Ellington plays at the Cotton Club.

These were the births:

- Hubert Taffin de Givenchy, French fashion designer
- Fidel Castro, Cuban revolutionary leader

Then Shirley added her comment: "Bob, this is the year *you* were born!"

For Bob's parents, 1927 was a year of both joy and grief. Harold Jr. became very ill with strep throat and died that year.

"King" Cotton

Harold was not satisfied—not even happy—in his role of teaching and coaching. His degree was really no help because of the limited number of available jobs. The family was growing, so Harold would have to find something that would meet their basic needs.

Floy, Flara's twin, had married an entomologist named Levi Curl. In fact, Levi was head of the Bureau of Entomology and Plant Quarantine of the United States Department of Agriculture (USDA), Pink Bollworm Division. At the time, the department was located in San Antonio, Texas, but would later move to Washington, DC. Levi asked Harold if he was interested in coming to work for his department. Some of the work was in Florida.

Levi's department was charged with the assignment of eradicating the pink bollworm, which was a serious threat to cotton crops across the entire United States. At that time, just prior to War World II, cotton was a major part of the American economy. It was "king" in many of the Southern states.

As early as 1917, pink bollworms were discovered in Texas. Pink bollworms are not the same as the boll weevil, which is harmful but can be eradicated if a farmer can afford the insecticide. The boll weevil originally entered the United States by crossing the Rio Grande River in about 1892 and then spreading rapidly throughout southern Texas. By 1922, it had infected 85 percent of the Cotton Belt. The insects punctured the cotton bolls and laid their eggs inside. Within a week, the eggs hatched into grubs that fed on the boll. The entire cycle from egg to adult was about three weeks, so as many as seven generations were possible in a single growing season. The grub-punctured cotton boll would either shed or not mature properly.

Although the boll weevil did considerable damage, some sort of a crop was still possible. But the pink bollworm would not allow a crop. The larva of the pink bollworm would burrow into a boll and eat all the cotton before the boll could ever open.

The USDA got the job of eradicating these destructive pests. The *Key West Citizen* newspaper reported a story about this threat in its November 21, 1935, edition:

> A small group of WPA workers was employed yesterday and today on the eradication of the wild cotton growth in Monroe County. Within the next few days 20 other workers will be assigned to the project at Tavernier and 20 at Key Largo.

There seemed to be two reasons for Levi Curl's department to concentrate on Florida. One was the belief that the boll weevil wintered in the Keys and then would swoop up to Georgia, Alabama, and Mississippi to ravage the cotton fields. Another reason was that the Florida Keys would provide a stepping-stone for the Caribbean island pink bollworm to migrate north to the US cotton fields. It was known that cold killed the US cotton plants and that the Keys did not have severe cold weather. In the Florida Keys, wild cotton grew all year long for years without dying and matured into huge scrub trees. That gave rise to concerns that the pink bollworm would have a perpetual home in the Keys.

Wild cotton is the prehistoric ancestor of our domestic cotton but of inferior quality for commercial use. Wild cotton cannot be spun. It is a scrub, growing to as much as 12 feet high. Just how that cotton originally got there is speculation, but some think it was brought over from the Bahamas.

Much of the areas in the Keys and South Florida were wilderness. There were few, if any, roads, but the Keys were generally accessible by water. The crews utilized quarter boats as work-crew quarters. They were living quarters built on available used river barges.

The work was done very seriously and with great care. Each crew, many from the Bahamas, consisted of one supervisor and seven or eight workers with machetes. They actually stretched strings to make straight paths across the Keys to form grids. Paths were then cut perpendicularly for a checkerboard effect, and every foot of every key was inspected for wild cotton. The cotton gangs, as they were called, systematically followed the crisscross grid paths, removing every cotton plant with poisoned roots. The plants were hauled into clearings, where they were burned. The work went on for years and resulted in the almost complete annihilation of wild cotton—and rattlesnakes.

With the discovery of the pink bollworm in 1932 on the lower Florida Keys, farmers realized that these perennial cotton plants were ideal hosts for the dissemination of an insect pest that might, in time, threaten the domestic cotton industry of the entire South. Steps were promptly taken to eradicate this type of wild cotton, with the work being relentlessly pushed for years by the Federal Bureau of Entomology and state inspectors cooperating in every way. Each state had its own regulations regarding what to do if a pink bollworm was found—just one pink bollworm. Texas decided it would mandate that the cotton stalks be plowed under by a certain date. If one pink bollworm was found in Louisiana, cotton could not be grown in that parish for five years. Inspectors had to be thorough and careful.

The USDA had developed a process to identify the pink bollworm. The larva of the common boll weevil and the pink bollworm looked amazingly alike. The larva of the boll weevil had four little dots on the top of its head. They were arranged in a sort of rectangle. The pink bollworm also had four dots, but they were almost a square. Inspectors had to send a suspected bollworm to Washington, DC for verification. Any agent who actually found a pink bollworm received a great deal of credit. That was the task that challenged Levi Curl's department.

Harold had proved his ability as a cook, and Levi gave him the chance to cook for the crews who were after the pink bollworm. Those crews had to go wherever cotton was grown and ginned, so they traveled a lot. The work was demanding, and they had to meet rigid schedules. Harold accepted the job, and in the early 1930s, he moved his family to San Antonio.

Because the job required moving so often, the family rented houses or apartments in the location of the latest assignment. Often while Harold was away, the family would return to Van Alstyne where the grandparents lived. If Harold was going to be in a place for several months, say three or four, the family would travel with him. In 1933, they traveled together to Marfa, Texas. Nancy, their only daughter, was born in Marfa. With the harvest completed there, Harold and his family moved back to Van Alstyne.

Bob benefited from the strong influences of both of his families. His grandparents inspired him with their ethics and attitudes. He admired their ambition and persistent dedication. He had seen—and was seeing—his parents' flexibility and readiness to adapt. He felt encouraged to think and explore. The variety of cultures and environments his family encountered in their travels stimulated his learning and attitude.

The next assignment in West Texas was at Fort Davis. Young Bob had an experience there that had a deep influence on his future. Harold woke Bob out of a sound sleep in the middle of the night to see a lighter-than-air craft as it drifted overhead. It was a dirigible, nearly 850 feet long, with all its lights on. It was moving at a rather low altitude, which was necessary because wind currents were very damaging to these crafts. Bob estimated that the craft couldn't have been more than 2,000 feet above them. As he watched it drift out of sight, he dreamed of a future when he might be able to build something like that.

The next year, Harold was assigned to Artesia, New Mexico. Since he would be there for some months, the family moved with him. For their living quarters, they rented a house that used to be a house for chickens. Oh, it had been cleaned out and somewhat refurbished, but it was still interesting. After completing each assignment, the crew would return to San Antonio, the southern headquarters of the Pink Bollworm Division of the USDA, to await reassignment. These were not, as Bob recalls, idle times.

Between assignments, Harold took his family camping. He found a very soft field of vines at one of their campsites. The family spent the night lying on those vines. They were abundant and real solid but also soft. Much to their surprise, they found that the vines were poison ivy. Nancy and Bob were allergic to poison ivy. They all had the worst imaginable case of poison ivy after lying all night long on those luxuriant vines. The family was headquartered in San Antonio at the time, and the doctors back then didn't know what to do with poison ivy. The family treated each other with calamine lotion. That is all they knew to treat it with. It was an excruciating

Bob, Charles, Nancy, and Scoots back in Van Alstyne

A flying dirigible

three weeks. It was so bad because the rash was solid, from the tops of their heads to the bottoms of their feet.

Flara's mother's sister, Florence, managed an apartment complex in San Antonio. It could be an advantage to Harold's family, as well as his aunt's, for the Welkers to move into the complex that Aunt Florence managed. Harold learned that Aunt Florence got some sort of commission for each apartment she rented. To their surprise, being kin made no difference to Aunt Florence. Since she got a commission for every three-month lease, she saw to it that Harold and his family moved out when their three months were up.

Harold's next assignment took him back to Florida. He had made several trips to Florida, but the family had not gone along. They had always returned to their extended families in Van Alstyne. But for this trip, the entire family went. Driving to Florida with three young kids in a non-air-conditioned car with no radio and traveling at a speed limit of 55 miles per hour was not a pleasure trip. The miles dragged on from San Antonio to Miami.

There was some work that interrupted their trip to Florida. They were given an assignment in Atlanta, Georgia. Harold found a boardinghouse that provided accomodations as well as meals for the family. Just across the road from their boardinghouse was a major train depot. Huge trains with gigantic engines would pull what looked like miles of cars onto the side tracks for sorting. Charles and Bob spent their days exploring these trains. To their amazement, no railway personnel ever confronted them. Harold was at work, Flara was busy at home, and these boys were having a great time.

With the assignment completed in Atlanta, the family continued on to Miami. Bob enrolled in elementary school in Miami. The year was 1936. These folks from Texas were quite impressed with the climate and aura of Miami. They had never before seen coconut trees growing along a sidewalk. There was more water there than they had ever seen.

The First Baptist Church of Miami gave big sugar cookies to the children who attended Sunday school. Bob never forgot those cookies. Sunday school was a sweet experience for the Welker children.

In Florida, Harold was responsible for feeding the USDA crews that worked in the Keys, the Ten Thousand Islands area, and the Everglades. The experience he had gained working with Grandfather Durning's crews proved handy for this important responsibility. When this assignment changed, Harold moved his family from Miami back to San Antonio. The First Baptist Church of San Antonio was the largest Baptist church in town, and the family began attending services there. Perry Webb was the pastor. He was an impressive figure and an exceptional preacher. Charles, Bob, and Nancy were all baptized into the membership of the First Baptist Church of San Antonio. (Maybe those big sugar cookies from Miami had some influence on these Welker children.)

Tom, the youngest of the family, was born while they were in San Antonio. When Flara told the family about the coming baby, Bob broke into tears. He was 10 years old. He cried, "We are going to starve!" After a short stay in San Antonio, the family moved to Brownsville, Texas. They were able to stay in Brownsville for three and a half years, their longest stay anywhere up to that time. Bob started junior high school in Brownsville.

Brownsville was the home of Fort Brown, which was initially called Fort Texas. It was established in 1846 as the first US post in Texas. Zachary Taylor was the commander of Fort Texas. The fort was renamed after Major Jacob Brown, who was killed in a battle during the Mexican-American War. In 1867, Fort Brown became a permanent fort under the command of Captain William A. Wainwright. On April 20, 1915, Signal Corps officers Byron Q. Jones and Thomas D. Milling flew a Martin T near the Mexico-Texas border. The plane was fired at by troops of Pancho Villa. One of the last mounted cavalry units in the US Army, the 12th Cavalry Regiment, was based at Fort Brown. The fort was used by the United States Army Air Force in 1943 for flexible gunnery training and then disbanded in February 1946.

One of the vast ranches the Welker boys explored in Brownsville was the Yturria Ranch. The ranch was more than 100,000 acres. It was established by Francisco Yturria who was born in 1830 in Matamoros, Mexico. He became the first Mexican citizen to own property in Texas. In cooperation with Richard King, the founder of King Ranch, Yturria founded the first railroad in South Texas. During the three and a half years they were in Brownsville, Charles and Bob spent many hours in and around Yturria Ranch. Bob entered high school while they were in Brownsville.

The stay in Brownsville ended, and the family returned to San Antonio. Bob was now old enough to get his Social Security card and officially enter the job market. He got a job with a local drug store. He delivered prescriptions on his bike, manned the soda fountain, and swept and mopped the floors (before the store opened and after it closed) for five dollars a week. He worked 70 hours a week for five dollars and was not allowed to keep any tips customers gave in appreciation for his deliveries.

Harold was directed to go to Florida, and the family returned to Van Alstyne. Bob was now in his sophomore year of high school. Harold, with his assignment completed in Florida, returned to move his family back to San Antonio, the southern headquarters of the USDA's Pink Bollworm Eradication Program. Bob enrolled in Edison High School. Bob had now been in a different high school each year of his high school education—three years, three high schools.

In 1944, Harold was transferred to Lubbock, Texas, where Bob graduated from Lubbock High School. Work had forced the family to move four times, and Bob had attended four different high schools. You might think the family could move during the summer. But no, sir. When the department said, "Move," Harold had to move. There was no waiting around for summer or any special time. Because of the job and the frequent moves, the children were always meeting new people in school. That didn't cause the family or the kids any problems at all because in those days, having a good job was more important than where you lived.

When Bob graduated from high school in Lubbock, he was assured he could attend Texas Tech. In fact, the Welkers lived just about a block from the college at that time. When Bob was in high school, if he had the option, he studied subjects that had to do with engineering and subjects such as math and biology. He didn't do well in English. He thought that if one could do well in math, one could make it in the world. Bob then learned (experience is a hard teacher) that history and English were far more important than math. In his words, "I had to pay the fiddler for thinking that English was not important."

Bob had his heart set on joining the Navy. War World II was raging, and Bob was determined to be part of the forces to preserve freedom for the world. It may have been in April that Bob graduated from Lubbock High School. In the early part of World War II, young men were often allowed to leave school early in order to help harvest the crops, especially cotton. Bob was only 17 when he graduated from Lubbock High School. His birthday was March 31, so he would need his dad, Harold, to sign him into the Navy. Harold didn't want Bob to go straight into the Navy. Bob was very disappointed that his dad would not let him join the Navy immediately after graduation.

After completing his senior year at Lubbock High, Bob went to the school to get his diploma and then returned home. Remember, he had attended four high schools before graduating from Lubbock High School. It was not a big deal for him to participate in some kind of graduation ceremony. In fact, his folks didn't even go to the graduation exercise. It was still daylight when Bob got home that Friday. It was just before noon. Standing on the front porch was Uncle Lev (Levi Curl). Bob was surprised to see his uncle because Uncle Lev's headquarters were in Washington, DC. Bob asked, "Uncle Lev, what are you doing here?" Uncle Lev replied, "Oh nothing, but what are you going to do now that you are out of school?" Bob said, "I'm going into the Navy." (Harold had not yet signed to allow him to enlist.)

Uncle Lev told Bob, "Before you join the Navy, I have something I want you to do for us." When he said "for us," Uncle Lev was talking about the US Department of Agriculture. A person really couldn't say no to Uncle Lev. Because Bob understood that about him, he didn't try to argue with him. Uncle Lev had a gin trash machine that had to be delivered to San Antonio by 8:00 a.m. Monday.

The government was strict about timetables. Bob had not driven more than 500 miles in his whole lifetime, and it was just less than 400 miles from Lubbock to San Antonio. Here was Bob on a Friday afternoon with an 8:00 a.m. deadline on Monday. He left Lubbock about 4:00 on Saturday afternoon and knew he would have to drive all night because of the distance. And the speed limit at that time was 35 miles per hour. One of Bob's first inventions (the first of many) was his attempt to drive down the road with one eye on driving and one eye sleeping. He did try this, and sure enough, both eyes went to sleep. Then all of a sudden, he hit a big bump. There were only a few fences in West Texas at that time. Bob had left the road and driven into the middle of a field, where he came to an abrupt stop. He didn't even know where the road was, so he followed his tire tracks back across the field, located the road, and resumed his trip to San Antonio. Bob finally arrived in San Antonio at about 4:00 or 5:00 Sunday morning and drove to Uncle Lev's house. The Curls weren't home because Levi was at work in Washington, DC. However, since Bob knew where they lived, he was able to drive to the house and take a little much-needed nap in their driveway.

Bob worked with the gin trash machine crew for three and a half months or so. The gin trash machine was developed and designed to find pink bollworms, not boll weevils. In the ginning process, cotton went through several cleaning processes. The crew Bob worked with wanted the very first cleaning. Three-man crews went out with the gin trash machine to the gins where cotton was being processed. These machines went all over the country wherever cotton was grown and ginned. A member of the crew would go out to the gin in the area where they were working and collect what was called the first cleaner trash. Gins could not refuse the request because these crews were representatives of the US Department of Agriculture. The big insignias on the doors of their cars identified them as part of the United States government.

The gin trash machine separated the cotton from the insects in the cotton. It was a pretty sophisticated machine. Usually, there was no more than a handful of insects that came out of an entire sample of first-cleaned cotton. The inspector would spend the whole day examining the trash that came from that first cleaning sample. It was very detailed work.

Bob's crew worked mostly in East Texas and some in Louisiana. When the ginning season was over, they drove back to San Antonio. Who was standing in the garage when they got there but the head of the department, Uncle Lev. Bob was surprised to see his uncle and asked, "What are you doing here?" Uncle Lev said, "Well, what are you going to do now?" Bob immediately said, "I'm going to get into the Navy." Uncle Lev said, "Well, before you go, I have a little project in Florida that I need you to help me with." Remember, this is the man to whom no one could say no.

There were two houseboats working in Florida looking to eradicate the pink bollworm. One crew worked the Florida Keys. The other went up the coast and worked in the Ten Thousand Islands area. Their assignment was to look for wild cotton. Cotton was able to grow wild in these areas because of the almost-tropical climate. It was called wild cotton because it grew without cultivation. Wild cotton was not suitable for consumer use. This wild cotton seemed like it would never die. Some of the trees were eight inches in diameter and had thousands of cotton bolls.

Some of the Keys were absolute jungles. Bob had to be especially careful because he was highly allergic to poison ivy. The very first day on the job, Bob's boss stepped over a rattlesnake. It was amazing how quickly the crews became able to train their eyes to locate wild cotton growing in the jungle. Some of it was only two to three inches tall.

They did find quite a lot of cotton, although none of the big trees. These trees had been eradicated earlier. Their maps dated from the 1930s and noted where the largest cotton trees had been taken out. There would be thousands of seedlings coming up where those trees had grown.

In the 1930s, it was discovered that the pink bollworm was migrating up from South America and wintering in the wild cotton. The pink bollworm must have a cotton boll to care for itself during the winter. There were thousands of these wild cotton plants in the Florida Keys where Bob was working. Maps had been produced that tracked the Keys, so the entire area would be scrutinized. Crews would follow these maps looking for wild cotton, being careful not to step on a rattlesnake. There were thousands of rattlesnakes in the Keys. Bob personally killed 53 rattlesnakes.

On the houseboat where Bob worked, there were six men. He was the only young man in the crew. He was the rookie. On Bob's boat, the cook was a five-star cook (to hear Bob tell it, he could have been employed by a luxury hotel anywhere). In Bob's estimation, he was the world's best cook. He must have been 70 years old, having worked past the government's mandatory retirement age. The cook did not work on the Keys. He did all the cooking for this crew. That kind of cooking had a great appeal to a young man just out of high school. At graduation, Bob wasn't as tall as his sister. He was a little guy. But with all that good cooking, he had grown to six foot one.

After completing his work in Florida, Bob went to rejoin his family, who had moved to Cuero, Texas. Harold took Bob to San Antonio right away and signed him up for the Navy. However, it would be two or three weeks before the Navy would call Bob up for basic training. So Bob took a job with the railroad. He worked for the railroad twice—this one time before going into the Navy and again after he returned from the Navy.

Bob in 1947, dressed for work with the USDA

Bob in his Navy blues

Bob served on minesweeper *YMS-67*, shown here tied up on the Yangtze River in Shanghai, China.

The Strong Right Arm

The railroad was shorthanded. They were just beginning to use machinery to do some of the manual labor. Bob worked on a section gang. There were eight people on the crew. Bob was the only one with freckles and red hair. He was given the responsibility of operating one of the new machines that was just being implemented. The older crew hands had little training and little interest in learning to operate this new machinery. One of the machines was a bolt tightener. When it became necessary to replace a section of track, the bolts holding the track together had to be broken loose. They were huge bolts that had to be loosened. With this new bolt tightener, the bolts could just be twisted off, which would be impossible to do with any manual labor.

Bob worked for the railroad for three and a half weeks. One of his jobs was to tamp the rock under the ties that supported the rails. This tamping was demanding work. The tamping rods used were heavy steel, 15 or so pounds. He was hefting that heavy rod and pounding it into the rock all day long. Bob was in good shape because of his work in Florida. He had used a machete when clearing brush while working in the Keys and had developed a very strong right arm. That arm enabled Bob to tamp and drive the spikes into the ties that held the rail in place. His right arm stayed strong for a long time. Later, when Bob was a student at Texas A&I—after his time in the Navy—he found he had little skill as a football player but was able to beat all the football players at arm wrestling.

When the Navy called, Bob boarded a train in San Antonio for his trip to San Diego.

Bob was selected for several new jobs in boot camp. He was designated as a platoon leader and selected as captain of the platoon basketball team. They played other teams of recruits. Bob estimates that there may have been 20,000 to 30,000 naval recruits in San Diego during the time he was in boot camp there. The winners of these games between recruits were granted liberty. Liberty was the prize. However, they were only paid $50 per month, and $6.40 was deducted for insurance. What could they spend on liberty?

One of the jobs Bob was chosen for was captain of the head. The head in naval parlance is the bathroom. Bob had a crew of 12 men assigned to him, and they were responsible for cleaning the heads every day. Every Friday, chiefs would come to inspect the heads to see how well the crew had done its job. The crew with the cleanest head was granted liberty on Saturday. Bob's crew got more liberty than they could use. They were so busy that they could hardly use all the liberties they had won.

When Bob got his crew, nobody knew anybody. The crew members were assigned to him. Many of the men were from the North and East and didn't know anything about cleaning bathrooms. Bob was shrewd enough to trade some of his crew for men from Texas and the Southwest. The captains from the North and East knew nothing about working with those men from Texas and the Southwest. From his time in Brownsville, Texas, Bob knew how to work with the men whose culture was so different from that in the North and East. Bob traded crew members, so he ended up with a crew of men who knew how to clean a bathroom. Nobody cared who was on whose crew. The crew Bob recruited through trades knew how to clean the head. The heads in the Navy were huge. There may have been 20 toilets in the head where Bob was captain. Bob's crew could polish the toilets, sinks, stalls, and floors to a high shine. His select crew never failed an inspection.

Bob was in boot camp three to four months. He had a friend there from back in Cuero, Texas. His name was Walter Pieper (pronounced Peeper). Walter was over 30, or at least 30, and though he had young children, he had been drafted into the Navy. He may have been (according to Bob's later memory) the only German in the world who didn't drink. Bob and Walter would go on liberty together. They would find a good place to eat, go to the zoo, and things like that. Walter was a really good man, and when boot camp was completed, he was assigned to an aircraft carrier.

Bob was assigned to go to platoon leaders school. But his heart was set on ship duty. He exhibited the determination that drove him later to become not only an engineer but also the founder of a company that would span the globe. Bob began making the rounds of authorities who might influence his assignment to a ship. No one seemed able to help, not even the chaplain. Finally, Bob went to see the base commander. It was a daring move for a mere seaman. His passionate plea for ship duty was finally granted, and Bob was assigned to *APA-98*, the USS *Dutchess*.

The very day Bob got on his ship, the war was declared over. By contract, recruits were required to serve one year and a day following their admission into the Navy. With the war over, Bob still had 11 months to serve. He went overseas in the American Area Campaign, the Asia-Pacific Area. On July 23, 1946, Bob was mustered out of the United States Navy at Camp Wallace, Texas. He had reached the level of coxswain while serving on three ships: the USS *Dutchess*, the USS *Hornbill* (YMS-371), and the USS *YMS-67*. He received the $100 mustering-out pay, $241.57 in last earnings, and $8.70 for travel expenses from Oakland, California, to Cuero, Texas.

The discharge papers for Robert Howard Welker note under job preference: college—engineering—Texas. Bob had a strong desire to become an engineer. In order to actualize that dream, Bob would need a college education. Armed with the G.I. Bill to help with the expenses of a college education, Bob initially visited Texas Tech University in Lubbock. It was too large for Bob's preference.

C3862873

Series C

Honorable Discharge

from the
United States Navy

This is to certify that

ROBERT HOWARD WELKER _____ a _____ COXSWAIN _____

is **Honorably Discharged** *from the* _____ USN PERSONNEL SEPARATION CENTER CAMP WALLACE, TEXAS

_____ *and from the Naval Service of the United States*

this 23 RD *day of* JULY 1946

This certificate is awarded as a Testimonial of Fidelity and Obedience.

_____
J. R. HUME, CAPTAIN, USN
COMMANDING

Engineer

Bob returned to Cuero to determine where to go to college. Brother Charles and sister Nancy were both interested in Texas College of Arts and Industries in Kingsville, Texas. Texas A&M-Kingsville, as it's known today, is the oldest continually operating institution in South Texas. The school was chartered in 1917 as South Texas Normal School. The opening of the school was delayed due to World War I. After the war, it was founded as South Texas Teachers College in 1925. The name was changed to Texas College of Arts and Industries in 1929. In 1967, the name was changed again to Texas A&I University. A&I became part of the Texas A&M system in 1989. The present name, adopted in 1993, is Texas A&M University-Kingsville. Texas College of Arts and Industries, as it was called when Bob enrolled there, was located in Kingsville, 40 miles southwest of Corpus Christi, 126 miles north of Mexico, and 126 miles southwest of Cuero, where the Welker family was living.

Bob was still determined to become an engineer. Perhaps it was the strong influence of his father. Harold had earned an engineering degree from Georgia Tech. As a math teacher, he helped Bob see the importance of math. Bob often recalled that evening when he and Harold saw that dirigible flying overhead at Fort Davis. He was intrigued by the sight and how it moved. Maybe someday he would design and build. Isn't that what engineers do?

Because Bob had had a fascination with aircraft from his early years, he hoped perhaps to do some work in aeronautical engineering. However, Texas College had nothing to offer in the field at that time. Instead, he enrolled in the School of Natural Gas Engineering. A degree in natural gas engineering and the size of the school were just what he wanted.

Bob as he entered Texas A&I

DUPLICATE RECORD

OF

Welker, Robert Howard

Surname   First Name   Middle Name

Cuero, Texas

Town   State

TEXAS COLLEGE OF
ARTS AND INDUSTRIES
KINGSVILLE, TEXAS

B-330-546-2500

Bob's Duplicate Record from Texas College of Arts and Industries.

In the summers between his college years, Bob worked for the United States Department of Agriculture surveying cotton insect infestation and studying the effects of various poisons on the insects that attacked the cotton crop. USDA headquarters was in Waco, Texas, at the government's experimental station. Bob was responsible for an area that was basically Northeast Texas. Included in this area was Honey Grove, where Harold had taught and coached while the family was young. Bob was able to meet some of the boys (now men) that Harold had taught while coaching and teaching in their school.

For about two months of that summer job, Bob and the others surveyed fields where cotton was being grown. When the cotton began to be harvested, there were no more insects to study. During the last month of the summer before returning to school, they would study the effects of various poisons on the cotton. Many of the workers at this experimental station were children of parents who also worked with the government.

The requirements for completing a degree in natural gas engineering included an extra semester of college. The degree required 155 hours of class work compared to 120 hours required for other degrees. There were about 20 classmates who graduated with Bob with degrees in natural gas engineering. As time went by, Bob would visit these classmates as customers for the products his future company would produce. Because of his contacts in his company and in the industry, Bob learned of job openings to which he could commend his former classmates.

Just prior to graduation, Bob applied for a job with the DuPont Corporation, which was opening a new plant in Victoria, Texas. The company had planned to employ five college engineering graduates, and Bob was one of the five selected. While waiting for this new job to start, Bob met a man he knew from Cuero who worked for the Tennessee Gas Transmission Company. Bob learned from a friend that Tennessee Gas had operations in Mexico as well as in the United States. This man was involved with the operations in Mexico. After learning about the scope of Tennessee Gas, Bob determined that this was the company he just had to work for.

So Bob composed a letter to DuPont, explaining that he had another opportunity. He really had no desire to work in a plant and was excited about the possibility of working in the field with pipelines. The principals at DuPont responded positively to Bob's letter. They recognized that he had a passion for this work and encouraged him to go after it.

Tennessee Gas dates back to the 1930s and was incorporated on April 1, 1940. Its purpose was to bring gas from Louisiana to the Tennessee Market by pipeline. Over the years, the name changed. In 1947, it became Tennessee Gas Transmission Company. That name was changed to Tenneco in 1966. At this writing, Tennessee Gas is part of the Kinder Morgan network.

In 1943, the demand for natural gas in the heavily industrialized Appalachian area of the United States was crucial. Local reserves and resources were declining. Industry, entrepreneurs, and the federal government were looking outside for the resources needed to keep defense plants operating.

When the United States entered World War II in 1941, promoters of Tennessee Gas were Wade Thompson, Curtis Dall, and Victor Johnson. In 1943, the Federal Power Commission designated Tennessee Gas's pipeline "vital to the war effort" and committed to issue the necessary certificates to build the pipeline if Tennessee Gas could come up with its share of the financing. If Tennessee Gas could not come up with it, the project would go to Standard Oil in New Jersey, a subsidiary of Hope Natural Gas, which already had made preparations, even as far as purchasing some right-of-way.

Tennessee Gas was depending heavily on the ability and connections of Victor Johnson, who was well known and respected. He had founded the Mantle Lamp Company and was a major stockholder in Tennessee Gas. Johnson was counted on to raise Tennessee Gas's portion of the budget for the project, but he died unexpectedly of a heart attack. With time running out and in real danger of losing the contract, Tennessee Gas was desperate for help.

The Chicago Corporation came to its rescue. Chicago Corporation already had extensive holdings in the Corpus Christi, Texas, area. If Tennessee Gas would give Chicago Corporation 90 percent of the company and extend a pipeline into the Corpus Christi area, Chicago Corporation would supply the money that Tennessee Gas needed to fulfill its part of the contract. On September 20, 1943, Chicago Corporation assumed control of Tennessee Gas. According to the agreement with the Federal Power Commission, natural gas had to be flowing to customers in the Appalachian area by the winter of 1944–1945.

Henry Gardiner Symonds became the new president of Tennessee Gas in 1943. He had experience having managed the holdings of the Chicago Corporation in Corpus Christi. Ray C. Fish, who, when working with Stearns-Roger Manufacturing, had designed a pipeline for the Chicago Corporation, served as vice president of engineering and construction for Tennessee Gas.

Facing labor shortages (they were prohibited from hiring anyone from another job), unusually severe weather, lack of equipment, and regulatory hurdles, Tennessee Gas still managed to complete the pipeline by the winter of 1944–1945. The project was completed on schedule and under budget. The pipeline was 1,265 miles long.

A.O. Smith Corporation and National Tube Company supplied most of the steel pipe. Merco-Nordstrom furnished the mainline valves. Worthington Pump & Machinery and Cooper-Bessemer Company built the 58 massive compressors (each powered by 1,000 horsepower). Stearns-Roger Manufacturing built seven original compressor stations, three types of gas metering stations, and a dehydration plant at Corpus Christi to remove water and impurities from the gas. Mainline block valves were installed every 10 miles in case they were needed.

Tennessee Gas's pipeline crossed 70 counties in seven states. It was the first in the world to be constructed solely with welds. Welding was cheaper, faster, and avoided the use of Dresser couplings and flanges. The first 1,180 miles of the pipeline used 24-inch pipe; the last 85 miles used 20-inch pipe.

Bob was excited about working for Tennessee Gas. His acquaintance from Cuero introduced him to W. C. Magee, a vice president at Tennessee Gas. Magee took Bob through Tennessee Gas and assured him that he would be able to find a place for Bob to work there. Bob was introduced to the engineers who seemed to be too focused on their own responsibilities to consider giving Bob a job. They were not very excited about finding a place for Bob to work. When Magee and Bob came to the survey department, Magee said to them, "You can use this guy, so find a place for him."

Bob's first job for Tennessee Gas was on a surveying crew near Corpus Christi, Texas. His crew was surveying areas for new pipelines to be constructed. His first day on the job, Bob broke his foot, the bone that goes to the little toe. Despite the injury, he learned how to walk without further injuring the break and thus never missed a day's work. He worked in the survey department for six months, but surveying was not the kind of job that fed Bob Welker's passion. Being a surveyor might be okay for some people, but it did not challenge him to fulfill his destiny. Bob was not happy surveying.

Magee told Bob that he would introduce him to various other departments in Tennessee Gas. The first department they visited was dispatching. Bob observed that dispatchers stayed in the office and had very detailed work. Dispatching did not interest him at all. However, the chief of the department later became president of East Tennessee Natural Gas Company. Dispatch sort of ran the details of the pipeline. Dispatchers had to keep an eye on the pressures in the pipelines. If there was some type of emergency, then dispatch would naturally alert the company.

The superintendent of dispatching introduced Bob to the assistant superintendent of gas measurement. Bob got him to explain what he does. The man worked with gas measurement and pressure regulation. In measurement, you're always on the move in the field. Measurement follows the pipeline in the assigned area. That is what Bob wanted to do.

Bob spent six months in the home office. He needed to become acquainted with the personnel and processes by which the company operated. While biding his time there, Bob met his future wife. Emil Farr introduced Bob to Shirley Rystrom, saying, "Bob, let me introduce you to your future wife." From time to time, Bob had the opportunity to talk with Shirley when he called in from the field on the telephone system owned by Tennessee Gas. Shirley had been at Tennessee Gas about a year and a half when she was introduced to Bob as "his future wife." Some years after their marriage, Thelma Farr, Emil's wife, told Bob that Shirley had said to her, "I sure hope he notices me." When later reflecting on their marriage, Bob said to Shirley, "We just seemed to get along perfectly from the very start."

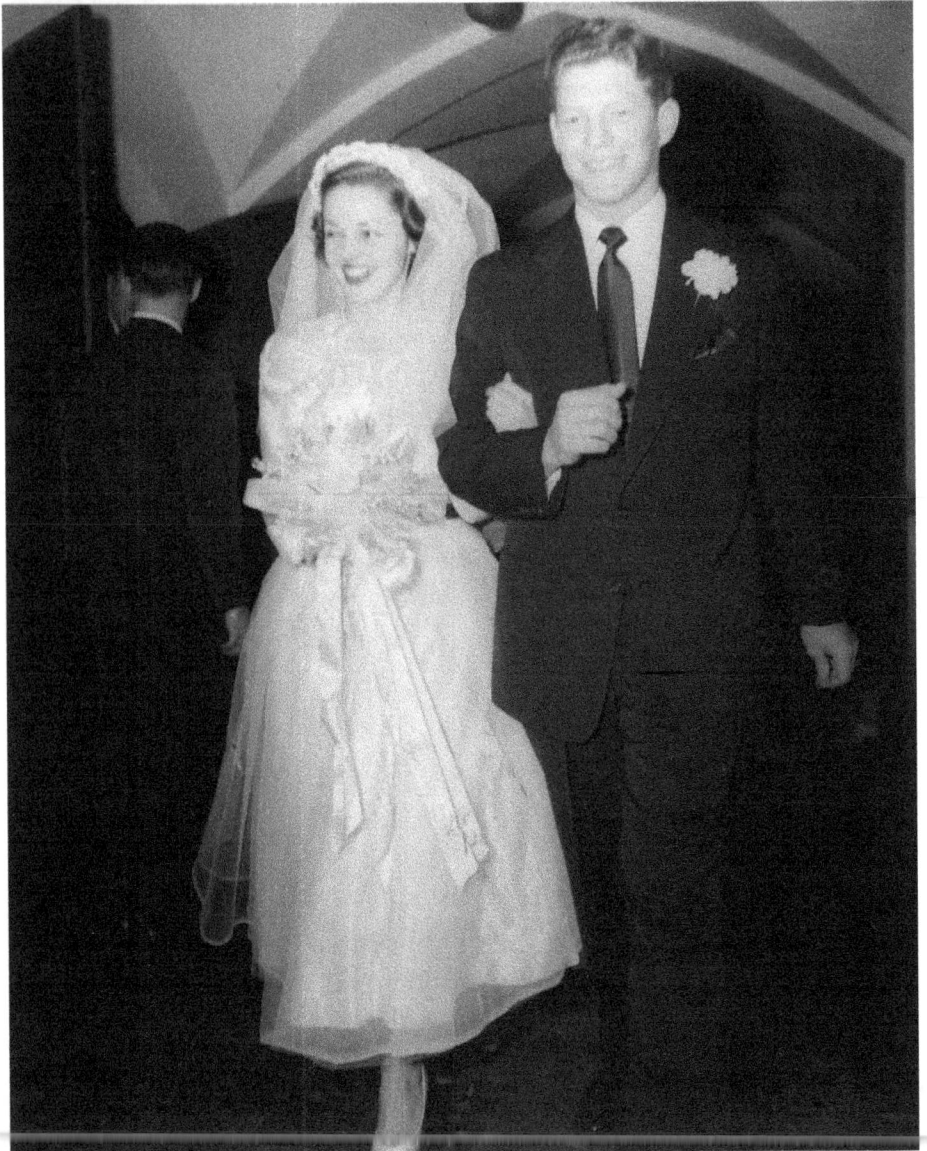

Bob and his new bride, Shirley

Bob was assigned to work with the new pipeline Tennessee Gas was building for New York and New England. The entire state of New York would be Bob's responsibility. The company had a rule not to exceed 50,000 miles on an automobile. Bob drove so much and put so many miles on the car that he got a new car about every 10 months. He was the only one in New York State that was in the measurement department of Tennessee Gas.

Bob and Shirley moved to New York after their wedding in December 1951. They rented a house in Richfield Springs, New York, in the Finger Lakes area of the state. It was a small house and very old. There were some places where you could actually see the great outdoors through spaces in the old walls. The house, their first, rented for $35 a month. Yes, $35. After Bob and Shirley rented the house for three years, the owner informed them that he was going to sell the house. For whatever reason, Bob never asked the price (which he would regret).

Bob and Shirley had to start looking for another house. Bob didn't say anything to Tennessee Gas about having to move. He found a house listed in the local newspaper. It was a small house located in Clifton Springs, New York, on the north end of the Finger Lakes. The house was being sold by the bank, which was taking bids. Bob bid $2,400. It was a prefabricated house and expertly built. It was fully insulated and even had natural gas plumbed in (the house they rented in Richfield Springs burned coal at first then oil). This house was less than 900 square feet, but it had a full basement, and the attic was finished. The lady that sold them the house worked in the local hospital. She was 96 years old, had never married, and worked until the day she died. Whenever a potted plant was left at the hospital, she would take it home and plant it in the yard. You couldn't even see the house from the street. The place looked like an arboretum. There were some really pretty trees in that yard, though, including a flowering cherry tree. It was full-grown and fully blossomed. But the lot looked like a jungle. When Bob and Shirley first walked up to the house with the representative from the bank, a grouse flew out of a tree near the house. "I just knew," Bob said, "that it was a sign that this was our house."

They got the house for their $2,400 bid. The G.I. Bill would help Bob with the mortgage because of his tenure in the Navy. With the government financing, the length of the loan, and the low purchase price, the monthly payments were only $18.

Their first child, Sherell, was born while they were in Clifton Springs.

One of the first things Bob did after they got the house was to get the compressor station to bring their equipment to their property (they had all the equipment necessary to maintain the pipeline, including bulldozers, backhoes, etc.) and uproot some of the trees that blocked the view of their house. They pulled up most of the pine trees.

Tennessee Gas put in measurement stations along the pipeline to log the flow of gas. Measurement stations (or metering stations) are critical because billing is based on the gas measured through the station. Metering stations are designed for the simultaneous, continuous analysis of the quantity and quality of the natural gas being transported through the line. Measurements identify the upper caloric value of the gas, which is the latent energy released during combustion. This metering value is the major variable when defining price. The presence of odorants is also noted. Tennessee Gas had a measurement station in Pittsfield, New York, near the Massachusetts border on New York State Route 22.

Route 22 goes out of New York City and follows the eastern border of the state. The route was established in 1930 as a primary route to Canada. It goes from the suburbs of New York City north to Mooers in Clinton County. At 337 miles long, Route 22 is the longest north-south road in New York State and the third longest overall.

Bob desperately needed someone to collect and mail the charts for him at this station near Pittsfield. All the gas going into New England came through this 24-inch pipe near Route 22. Getting an accurate reading on the measurement was crucial. Because it was winter, the locals weren't really interested in a job. These workers had an agreement with the state concerning inclement weather. When it was too bad to work such as during the winter, the local work force had allowances that carried them through. Nobody seemed the least bit interested in working a job that would take them out in the weather.

It was essential that Bob find someone to change charts at this strategic station. It was a real problem. Bob met Mr. and Mrs. Jean Ponsolle when they were out in their yard. As Bob visited with them, he told them he was looking

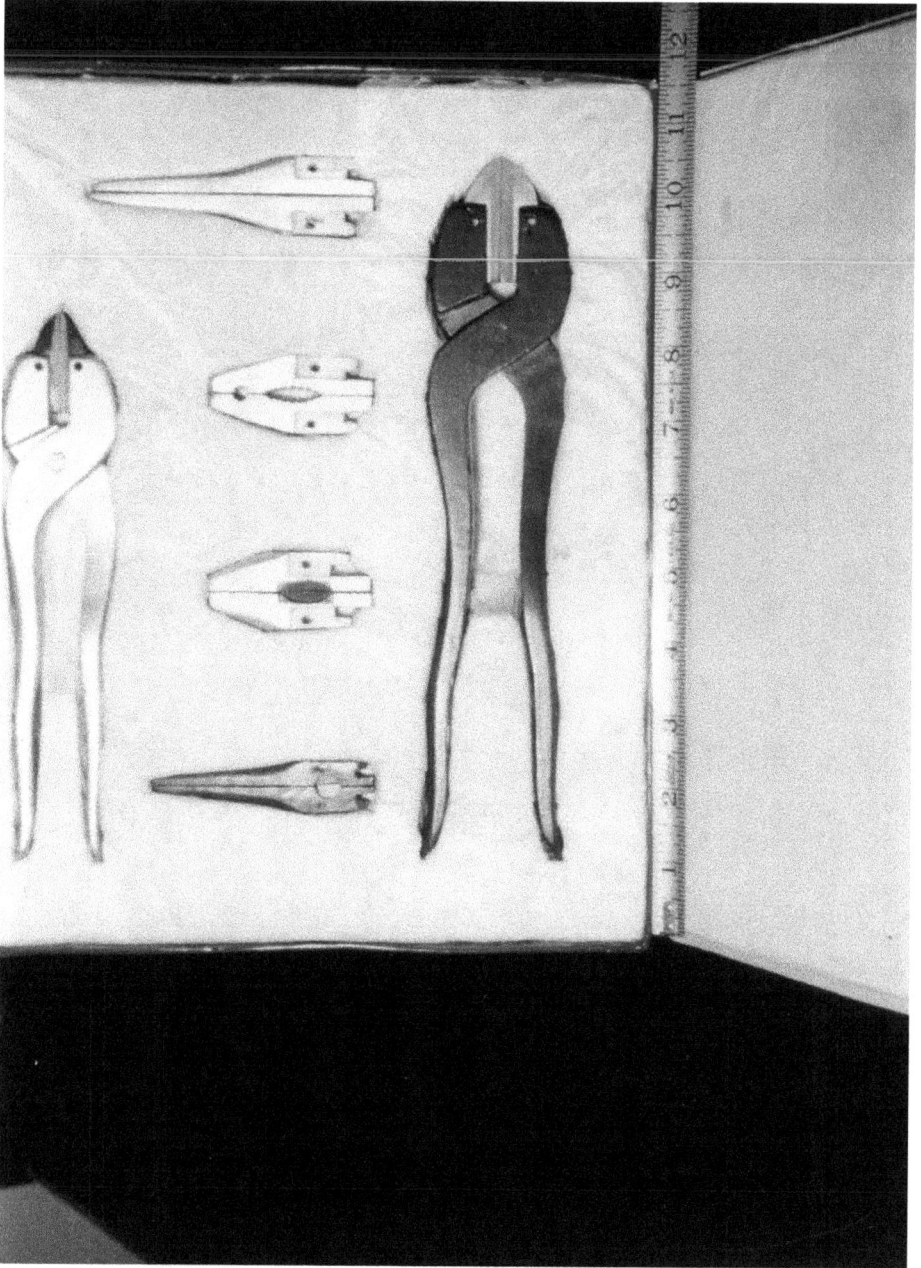

A plier that had interchangeable heads

A golf cart that could care for children. Note the faces of Sherell and Brian.

for someone to work with him, changing charts in the measurement station being located there. How was he going to find someone—anyone—to do this necessary work? Mrs. Ponsolle said, "Jean [her husband], you can do that."

Jean had been in World War I. He had been shot two or three times. Before they came to New York, Mrs. Ponsolle had been the cook at an exclusive establishment in Paris. In New York, she cooked for a customer who became a regular. He was an older man who had no family. For years, he had been eating at the establishment in New York State where she cooked. He was very appreciative of Mrs. Ponsolle's cooking, so much so that he said to her, "You go upstate and find us a place to live, and I will buy it. You cook for me until I die, and everything I own I will leave to you." Mrs. Ponsolle found a little hotel, which the man bought. He did not rent the rooms out. It was just where they lived until the man died. This man who had taken such an interest in Mrs. Ponsolle's cooking owned a lot. In fact, he owned five big warehouses in Philadelphia.

The Ponsolles bought a little house on the side of a mountain in the Catskill Mountains. Behind their house were tombstones that dated back to the Revolutionary War.

Jean was probably about 65 years old at the time he began working with Bob. He turned out to be a very determined worker. There were times when Route 22 was so covered with snow that you couldn't use your car. Jean would walk in the snow from his house to the station, maybe a couple of miles. Timing was very important in changing the charts, and Jean always made sure that, despite the weather, he was there when he needed to be there—always on time.

Mr. and Mrs. Ponsolle treated Bob like a son. Bob could usually be back home at night. However, when schedule or time dictated—and Bob was in the Pittsfield area—he would visit with the Ponsolles. You could not go to their house without agreeing to eat. It didn't matter if you had just eaten, you had to eat again. Mrs. Ponsolle was more than your average cook. She would buy a whole backstrap from the meat market from which she would custom-cut her steaks. She could really cook, and her bread was incredible.

The Ponsolles' house

Bob and Shirley were in New York for five and a half years. Sherell and Brian, their second child and only son, were both born in Clifton Springs. Another daughter, Mindee, was born after Bob was transferred and the family had moved back to Texas. Because Bob was a veteran of the Navy and because of his job move, he was qualified to purchase another house that the government would finance. The family settled in Richmond, Texas.

Bob became an area supervisor in measurement, responsible for three zones that extended from East Bernard to the Red River, with a man assigned to each zone. These men looked to Bob for whatever help they might need in their specific area of responsibility. Bob was constantly thinking about ways to do his work more effectively and improve the processes in the industry. One of the issues he was concerned about was the control valve.

Sherell and Tex peering out of the doghouse Bob built while the family was living in Clifton Springs, New York.

A map Bob designed to allow the family to follow his trips

Sherell, Brian, and Mindee in front of their house in Richmond, Texas

The Welker Jet Stream

The control valve regulates the flow of gas through the pipeline to meet the specifications and capacities of the meter. Control valves (also called regulators) are essential for the transmission of gas through a pipeline. Every pipeline has control valves. The valves used in most pipelines were built by Fisher.

William Fisher became the chief engineer of the city of Marshalltown, Iowa, in 1876. A raging fire broke out that threatened to destroy a major part of the town. Fisher was called to help maintain pressure on steam-driven pumps that projected water onto the fire. The fire was brought under control, but Fisher, exhausted by his long night of manual efforts, was inspired to discover some valve that would do what he had been forced to do manually. In 1880, he developed the Fisher Type 1 constant pressure pump governor. The device was granted patent number 305,167 in 1884.

As Bob worked and traveled, he was constantly thinking about ways to improve this control valve. He recalled how a packer was used in blowout preventers. It seemed to him that there must be some way he could utilize this packer to improve the control valve.

Necessary to production in the gas and oil industry was the blowout preventer, or BOP. So much is invested in drilling and the pressures are so high that some device was necessary to deal with emergencies that might arise during the drilling process. In 1922, Cameron Iron Works got a patent on a Ram-Type BOP. It was designed so a wedge could be rammed across the pipe, either shutting off the flow or, if necessary, cutting off and sealing the drill casing.

In 1946, Granville Sloan Knox invented a BOP that utilized a packer. This packer, an elastomeric packing unit, was basically a donut-shaped rubber seal. In the event of an emergency, a hydraulically applied piston would force the packer to seal off the pipe, including whatever was in the pipe at the time such as a drill stem. Knox received a patent on his invention in 1952. In 1972, Ado N. Vujasinovic was granted a patent for a modification he called Spherical BOP. It was this packer that Bob considered an innovation that would greatly improve the control valve.

While Bob was working in New York, the state passed a regulation that pipelines had to be tested hydraulically before being put into service. The testing process had to exceed the pressure under which that pipeline would normally operate in order to prove it was safe to transmit gas. The company did its hydrostatic testing with water from the river. However, with that water came a great deal of sand. When the water was flushed from the pipeline, much of the sand remained in the pipe. When gas began to flow, the sand was blown and cut into the valve seat of the control valves. Gas flows out of the control valve at the speed of sound. You can imagine the corrosive and abrasive effect that violent blowing sand had on the control valves. The valves were being cut by the velocity of the sand, which required unexpected maintenance and early replacement. Bob realized that this packer that was being used so effectively in the drilling processes could work well in the control valve he envisioned. Bob's idea was a valve that would permit the gas to flow straight through (without any interference) and utilize a rubber valve that would be less affected by abrasion.

In 1958, Bob submitted a patent for the Welker Jet Stream. This valve would use a rubber-plug-type plunger that was made of Buna-N rubber. This rubber is not as affected by abrasion as steel or some other type of valve seat. The patent application went through and was granted on the first offering. The Jet Stream was the first of Bob's several patents.

The Welker Jet Stream was tested in Louisiana and exceeded expectations. It proved to be less affected by abrasion. Several other features emerged, features that had not been offered before and are not duplicated to this day. The Jet Stream was the most innovative design of a control valve in more than 100 years.

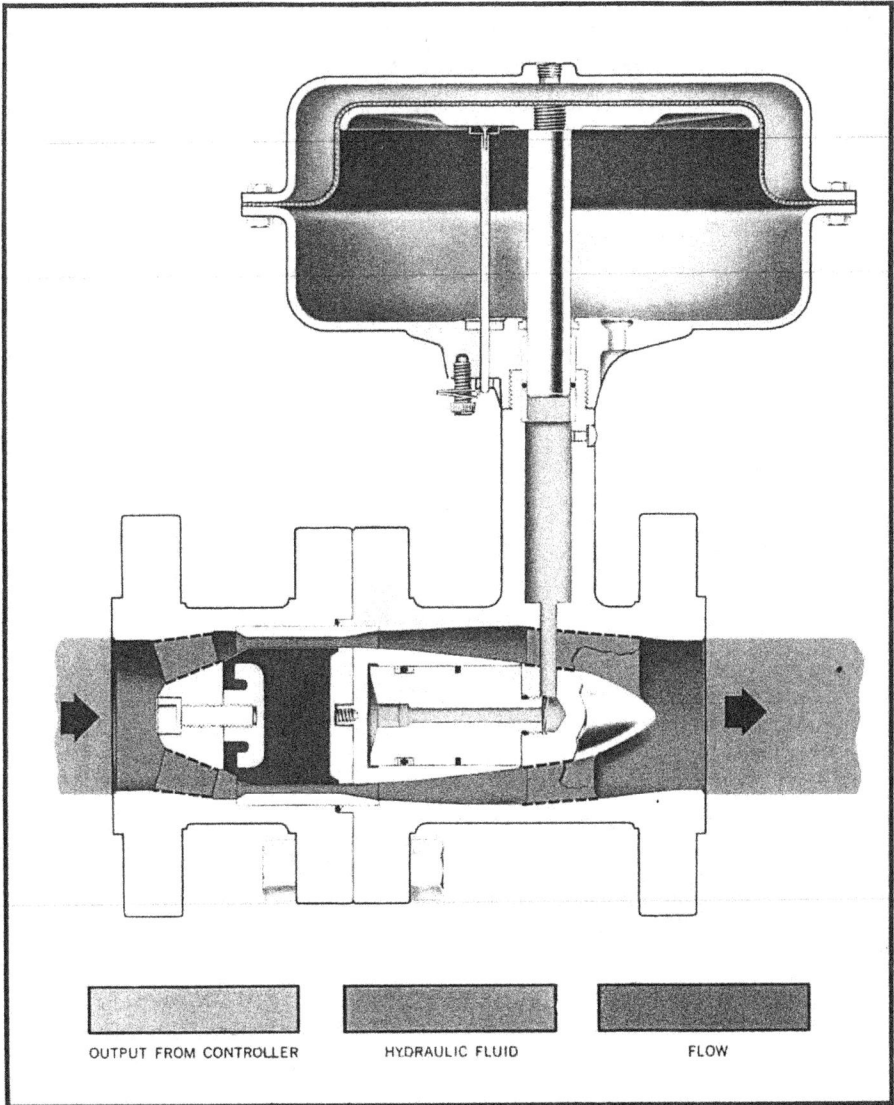

OUTPUT FROM CONTROLLER   HYDRAULIC FLUID   FLOW

Schematic of the Welker Jet Stream

Bob came up with an idea for improving the control valve and built a prototype while working for Tennessee Gas in East Bernard. He went to the company and explained that he was resigning in order to open his own company to sell his new regulator. He showed them the Jet Stream he had designed. Tennessee Gas bought Bob's first two regulators after he submitted his resignation but while he was still employed.

Hi Mom and Dad,

I wanted to take a few moments and write down some thoughts I have, so here goes.

This year has been challenging in many ways besides business, there was my knees and the challenge they presented to myself, Denise and my kids, then sweet Dolores passed away after a hard fought battle with cancer. But the good things also occurred, my recovery keeps getting better, we know Dolores is at peace with God and will see her again someday, Josh's family continues to grow blessing us with fun little grand kids, and Ellis is engaged, and it appears Kyle and Yo may be soon also, Tiff loves school and the life she has found up in Sooner land, and now you've turned the company over to me. WOW !

I wanted to let you know that I deeply appreciate your turning the Company over to me completely and making me Chairman of the Board. This shows me that you have the ultimate confidence in me, and decisions I make. Of course, I had great parents teaching me and guiding me during prior years ! I will continue to make pretty conservative decisions and of course, anytime I have a question I need your help on, I will ask. It feels very good to have parents I know I can talk to anytime. When I think back on the day you made me President back in 1983 (I was only 28), I must admit, I was very nervous and thought it was to early, but due to the way you raised me I stepped up and did pretty darn good, considering the industry crashed right at that time. It forced me to make decisions I did not know I had in me. I do know the good Lord was looking over my shoulder and guiding me the whole way !

Now, I am looking forward to making Josh the President of Welker sometime in the near future and giving him the same chance I had. I know he will step up to the challenge also, as he feels he was born to run this company and make it prosper. He is very conservative and thoughtful in his decisions and consults with me all the time. So I have no fear he will run off and make any "big" decisions without my approval. He has a wonderful, supporting family behind him, and this will only help him in future decisions he will have to make.

Kyle also has certainly stepped up with Odoreyes and taken charge, so he could have some very good things happening for himself also. I know once he marries Victoria it will add to his stability as a business manager, as a good woman always helps a decent man become better !

Ellis is beginning to think Flow has more potential now as he learns more, so he may really begin to take charge there as the year goes forward. We will see as time progresses, but Flow could very easily be a company we sell if we capture a few of the big jobs that are under consideration right now. Regardless, Flow can hold it's own as it grows along.

Daniel is still searching for "the right spot" for himself, he is very comfortable with Josh, so that may just work out right, but I know he wants to be in charge of his destiny deep down inside.

All four boys are very comfortable talking to people in this industry, something they got from their mom, which is very neat to me. Especially Kyle, he really looks forward to learning more and more so he can give better and better talks.

All in all, it is near impossible for me to think of words to thank you for the opportunity you have given me through the years with Welker, the basic words "thank you" don't seem enough – but I want you to know they come from deep in my heart. When I was a youngster, I thought many times you were to hard on me, but now I know they helped form the basic character I have now. I definitely feel with hard work, perseverance, and God in my heart anything can be accomplished, and I thank you for instilling that into me. I know there were times you probably thought "what is this kid doing", but you both are always in my thoughts as I make decisions. For this, I am very grateful.

Mom and Dad, I love you very much, and look forward to the future with wide open eyes, and desire for success and growth. I also look forward to being able to come out occasionally and spending time with you guys this next year and years to come !

I started at writing this, but I kept changing things, so I decided to type it. It still contains all my love and feelings I have for you both!

I Love you
Brian

A letter from Brian

Welker Engineering

Bob began his own company, Welker Engineering, in the garage of his home in Bellaire, Texas. The big stuff was farmed out to machine shops. These shops needed work because the oil patch was down. One shop that Bob used wanted him to take some of the $18,000 he and Shirley had saved during the six years in New York to buy 25 percent of the company. Even before they began talking about such a deal, Bob was allowed to come in at night and do work in the machine shop as long as the machines were cleaned up when they came in to work the next morning. There were times Bob would come in at 2:00 in the morning and work until the employees came at 8:00. Bob was machining other devices he had developed and selling a few of them. He did not follow through on the offer to buy 25 percent of the company.

There were some uneasy moments because Bob was a registered engineer, and many of the engineers in the companies where he worked were not. Bob never made an issue of it, but many of the engineers took it the wrong way. However, after Bob left Tennessee Gas, some of the engineers who had had uneasy feelings about Bob being a registered engineer became some of his best friends. From time to time, Bob would have issues with the chief engineer at Tennessee Gas. Bob was careful to never be too critical, but the disagreements were real. You see, one of Bob's responsibilities was to take the things the chief engineer had designed and make them work. Sometimes, what he had designed just wouldn't work.

There is an annual school dealing with the natural gas industry. The school convenes at the University of Oklahoma (OU) in Norman, Oklahoma. While visiting some of his competitors at OU, Bob met a man working with the Accessories Product Company (APCO) in Fullerton, California. The representative had been assigned to find a regulator that APCO could manufacture. APCO had a history of building regulators for liquid fuel rockets. With the advent of solid rocket fuel, its regulators would be in less demand. The representative was very interested to learn more about Bob's regulator. Bob had taken a regulator to the school but due to protocol was not allowed to bring it to the school. "Do you have one of your regulators here?" the APCO representative questioned. When he saw the Jet Stream, he was sold. He immediately called the California office to tell the company he had found exactly what they were looking for.

APCO asked Bob to visit company headquarters to talk about his regulator. The family went along, and the trip extended to two weeks. APCO was solidly impressed and agreed to buy the patent for the Jet Stream. It wasn't an amicable decision. The engineering department protested—loudly. "We could design a regulator just like this," they griped, "and you have gone out and bought a design without consulting us." The whole department threatened to quit. When their ultimatum was brought to the administration, administration said, "Go ahead and quit." The engineers didn't quit. APCO did manufacture the Jet Stream, though the engineers there were a constant challenge.

Bob was out of money. He and Shirley had used up their savings. Now they had children, no jobs, and only what Bob could earn with his mind and energy. The patent was sold to Accessories Product Company for $5,000.

Platt Turner, the president of Texsteam, a company owned by the Vapor Corporation of Chicago, went to the same church as Bob and Shirley. He was a real nice man and sort of the head deacon at the church. Bob called him one day, and they began visiting. In his responsibilities with Texsteam, Turner worked with Tennessee Gas and knew that Texstream was interested in Bob's regulator.

Bob's arrangement with APCO was not working out. APCO was willing to sell the patent for the Jet Stream to Texsteam, which would manufacture Bob's regulators in its gigantic machine shop, and Bob would be their sales representative. Bob didn't ask for any money up front. He only asked for the typical 5 percent royalty for each regulator he sold. Bob's first order of regulators was with the Natural Gas Pipeline of Chicago. The order was for 99 regulators. What a start!

Bob had some issues with the engineers at Texsteam, as he did with the engineers at APCO. The engineers at Texsteam changed rubber companies, which affected the quality of his regulators. The rubber used to construct the inner valve in the Jet Stream had to be very high quality. The best Bob had found was made by a company run by F. H. Maloney. However, Maloney went out of business, and that made finding an adequate replacement difficult. Over the years, Bob's company worked with more than 20 different rubber companies. It became an ongoing search.

Letters Home: A Man's Soul

Most of Texsteam's products were being sold through large ware-house-type stores in the United States. Bob was the only one of Texsteam's staff who was selling the Jet Stream in Europe. On Bob's first trip to Europe, Andy Watson, a representative of Texsteam, went along to introduce Bob to principals in the gas industry there. They flew first to New York and then on to London. After that, Bob made extensive trips to Europe.

Gas had just been discovered in the North Sea, and pipelines were brand-new in Holland. Bob would have to make trips back to these customers to help train them in the use of his regulators. They loved Bob's equipment because it would do what they needed without them having to do it, and they became technically adept in using it.

On these long trips that took Bob away from his family, he wrote home almost every day. The letters now provide a rich view into the heart of a man who was dedicated to his Lord first, his family second, and his job third. When he wasn't making presentations to prospective clients or resting, Bob was searching the area for gifts and mementos he could send back home. His letters served as a sort of tour guide for the folks back in Texas.

In one of his letters in 1964, Bob described to his family some keen information about the windmills in Holland. He explained that the position of the blades signaled information to the countryside. One position communicated, "All right." Another said, "Send help." And yet another announced, "Mill not operating."

Bob was in Germany in 1966 to demonstrate the Jet Stream. He had noted that the popular regulator with the German industry weighed six to

10 times what the Jet weighed, and it was very noisy, much more so than the Jet.

In that same letter, Bob shared with his family, "When things get rough is when a person begins to feel like he is all alone. Thank goodness we need never to be alone."

In one of his meetings with the German industry, Bob was the only English-speaker in the group. He had to rely on a good interpreter who knew English well but knew nothing about a regulator.

Timing was just right for the Jet Stream and its eager developer. Bob noted in a letter dated March 4, 1966, that "70 more stations were to be built in Holland." Reflecting on the regulator, Bob wrote, "Oh yes, the regulator (a gift from God, I believe, because I never set out to think up a new regulator. It just popped into my head and then we had the chance to make something of it)."

Writing home on March 6, 1966, Bob said, "God has given each of us a great deal. What shall we do in return?" The next day, he sent home another piece of solid counsel: "The important thing is not to compromise what you believe in for the sake of getting along."

A letter he wrote on April 30, 1967, revealed Bob's heart. Here is an excerpt from that letter:

> You know, I think often of God's grace in our own lives and it causes me to stop and reflect on the fact that it is God who in kindness and mercy has given us to one another for a season. "What's this about a season?" you say. Well now, in Ecclesiastes 3:1 it says, "To everything there is a season." Mainly we want to be thankful that we can look forward to that season that has no ending. This is with our Lord Jesus.
>
> Brian and Mindee you should think about your relationship to Jesus. Did He die on that cross for you? Mother and Sherell and I can pray with you that God would open your heart to the Savior and when you are alone you can ask God to show you what must be done in your life.

Here is an excerpt of a letter sent home from his stay in the Grand Hotel Central in The Hague. Apparently, Bob had gotten word from home that the children were "pretty good." Here is Bob's response:

It was with great disappointment to have Mother tell me "well, pretty good" when I asked how you had been acting. When I leave home for a hard trip is the best I can expect just "pretty good"? Don't you know that I expect you to be absolutely good when I am away? I need to know that you are doing everything possible to make things easy on Mother and listen my friends it is not just for Mother that I expect you to do right, it is for your own character building. Now (NOW) is when you build character, not when you get grown. How do you show good character building progress at your young age, you might ask? In thousands of ways: by obeying promptly, by taking care of your studies, by taking care of your room, your clothes, your yard, your appearance, your health. There are countless other traits I could mention but let me end by saying that when you neglect any of the above efforts (and they will have to be planned efforts on your part) both Mother and I take note of it and while we may not always say something to you we are disappointed because you will again have failed to stand up to the God-given responsibilities that are being given you. Naturally Mother and I will be doing our best to help you make the right decisions and we will have to punish you from time to time for getting out of hand, as children will do, but the test is not with Mother and I, it is with each of you, and we should all pray that God will guide you to develop a strong, reliable character.

About his trip to Frankfurt, Germany, Bob wrote, "The bedrock of the Natural Gas industry is Europe."

Bob's work with what he accepted as a gift from God—the Jet Stream—is described in Ecclesiastes 9:10: "Whatever your hand finds to do, do it with all your might." Even while engrossed with a very heavy schedule abroad, Bob noted in a letter dated October 7, 1964, that he had written to 24 customers in the United States. He was determined to make the best of the opportunity God had given him.

While doing his work with the Jet in London, Bob noted that his English hosts referred to the Jet as a "jewel" and called it a "frightfully clever device." In France, the Jet was tested against and with a Fisher valve. The Fisher valve was already in service there. The Jet clearly impressed the French. Bob was so impressed by the comparison with the Fisher valve that he wrote in a letter back home, "Just think, one day it [the Jet] may be the standard of the industry."

On this trip, Bob went to Australia. After he landed in Melbourne, he wrote the folks back home that being there was "like going to Brownsville [Texas] for a month."

On a side note, in 1966, Bob returned to some of the places he worked with two years earlier. He had first-class reservations for his trip to London. As he was waiting at the terminal, Bob noticed a crowd around a celebrity making his way to the first-class section of the plane. When Bob entered the plane, he was informed that his first-class seat had been given to that celebrity. The celebrity was Cary Grant. Yes, Cary Grant bumped Bob from his reserved seat. The flight crew tried to make compensation. Bob was given a whole row of seats (three across) with this perk: "You can lie down to sleep as we cross the ocean." Bob and Cary got to London—one in business coach, and one in first class.

On this trip, Bob wrote a letter home dated March 9, 1966: "God doesn't just answer prayers for preachers, but hardware salesmen as well!! I have noticed that when I am confronted with a hard job; if I say an earnest prayer, asking for 'backbone' no less, it is always given and that job will fall right into place."

Remember Bob's statement about the bedrock of the natural gas industry in Europe? Well, in Holland, for example, Bob's first order for the Jet Stream was for more than $600,000.

The love and care Bob had for his family he had to leave in Texas was expressed in letter after letter. He was feeling deep appreciation when he wrote to the kids, "Treat your mother just like she is a gift from a sovereign God, because she is." Also aimed at the children, he wrote, "But what we want is for you to prepare yourselves for a good life after school is behind you. You see, what we do with the talents God gives us can reflect glory to

Him and if by His grace the talents are developed, then we know that He has given us a special gift."

Visiting with the kids about goals, Bob wrote, "To do your best in what you are truly happy doing. Do that and all the success you will ever want will pursue you like old age. Inescapable!"

On a return trip to Holland in 1971, Bob learned that $7.3 billion was to be invested in the natural gas business over the next three years. Thinking of that marvelous gift—the Jet Stream—Bob stated, "How is it that the Jet Stream is our idea? By the grace of God."

While in Brussels in 1971, Bob wrote home about values and endeavor:

> There is a mighty fine happy life potential represented here and we should always ask God to help us make the most of it. Did you know that anyone can be mediocre or do nothing? God's Word tells us to run the race to win. If then, we don't win, then knowing that we did our best is actually just as good. Can that be? Assuredly, because we are not really racing against people with our lives. We are racing against the devil. He says, "sit down," "no need to try," "quit," "cop out," "flake off," and God has told us in ages past that we are equipped to do good, so strive.

Texsteam was manufacturing the Jet Stream, but it was not all that careful about the work. More than once, orders were delayed. Work without real care meant regulators that were not up to specifications. Bob was learning a lot about running a business from his experience with Texsteam (both positive and negative), but he was concerned about attention to essentials.

Texsteam sold the patent for the Jet Stream to Welker Engineering. The company seemed glad to be rid of it. Bob was grateful to have more control of it. Though Bob had worked with Texsteam for 13 years, they proved to know little about his regulator. In fact, Texsteam filed a lawsuit against Welker Engineering concerning the Jet Stream. Bob asked his attorney to question the chief engineer at Texsteam. On the stand, the engineer was asked, "Which direction does gas flow through a regulator?" He could not answer that basic question.

In the 13 years Bob was with Texsteam, he estimated that he may have sold thousands of his regulators. He was paid a five percent royalty for each regulator sold. At the time, royalties were paid for 17 years. If alterations were made to a patent, the royalties could extend to 20 years.

**OBAN
ENERGY SERVICES
PTY. LTD.**
(Inc. in Vic.)

14 Waterdale Road, Ivanhoe Vic. 3079
Phone (03) 499 3879   Fax (03) 499 7612
Correspondence to:
P.O. Box 5020 Alphington Vic 3078 Australia

16 July 1996.

Dear Bob,

Last week I remitted funds to Welker Engineering Co for the
last time,and so concluded six and a half years as Welker
Control Valve representative in Australia,through my own
company.

Having done that I began to think nostalgically of the
personal and professional association I have had with you
since 1968 when you made your first visit to Australia.

Since that time,my life has been, in so many ways,influenced
by your wise counsel and practical assistance,and there is
so much for which I must express my thanks and appreciation.

In 1968 you taught me,among many things,that there was more
to gas distribution than cast iron pipes carrying gas at
about 4 oz./sq in- hence the need for equipment such as the
'Jewel'.(I still have,on my office wall,the framed coloured
photo of the Jetstream as well as a small black and white
photo of a very young Bob Welker with a four inch Jet.)

I recall your efforts to successfuly keep the Jet agency
with AAEC rather than have it go to the American Meter rep.
This was probably the most vital action which kept AAEC afloat
-it could not have survived with-out Texsteam account.That
is for sure.

At the end of your two weeks visit you could see that AAEC
needed more agencies and you steered Anderson Greenwood and
Robinson Orifice in our direction. AGCO went on to become
the flagship for AAEC and Robinson,indirectly led us to
Mercury Instruments which became another 'boomer' and led
us into the world of metering -particularly with Turbine
meters.

In 1969,I know that you were largely responsible for getting
me over to the USA for my first overseas trip,and this
experience really opened my eyes as to what the gas industry
was all about.

When you got WEC up and running and producing the Welker Jet,
you saw to it that we (AAEC) would have the agency and for
this we were most grateful-even when the son took over from
the founding father of AAEC and decreed that all accounts
would be payable in 150 or more days,you stayed with us.

(2)

When it became obvious to me at the end of 1988,that AAEC was
totally unviable (although the Mackenzie clan would not admit
and face up to it),I had to get out, and it was then that I
set up Oban Energy Services doing consulting work,
After twelve months,when AAEC finally'went down the gurgler',
you did not hesitate to offer me the Welker account for
Australia - and so began the six and a half years which has
been the most interesting,satisfying and rewarding period of
my professional life.

I believe that David has advised you that I have been diagnosed
as one in a thousand,world wide , who contracts Parkinson's
disease and,mainly for this reason,I have decided that now
is the time to 'call it a day' and have some holidays which I
have not had for about nine years.

I guess we can all say 'what if?' I can say "what if I had
never met Bob Welker?' I'm sure that my life would have been
very different, but I'm equally sure that it would never have
been as satisfying and fulfilling.

As you know Bob,I do not share many of your personal beliefs,
but I do admire you for your resolute Christian witness and
unbending faith. I sometimes wish I could have faith in a
supreme being,such as you and Shirley (and my two sisters)
have, but it is not for me,at this time,at least.

Well my friend,I hope you and Shirley live long to enjoy the
fruits of your brilliant career.
Please accept my undying gratitude for the part you have
played in my life.

Yours most sincerely,

John McDougall.

Letter from the area representative in Australia

Time for Everything

When Bob left Texsteam, Welker Engineering consisted of Bob, his brother Tom, and some machinists. Welker Engineering was first located in Bob's home garage. One day, Bob was having lunch in a café by the ship channel in Houston. That's a long way from Bellaire, which is on the other side of town. He heard a couple of men talking over their lunch and recognized that they were lawyers. They were talking about some man in Bellaire who was running a business from his home. Bob realized they were talking about him. He went straight home and moved everything out of his garage that very evening. He found a tiny little shop just down the street from where he lived and rented it. Being able to avoid any legal action from these lawyers assured Bob that God was looking out for him.

Bob also located a two-story building where he could store his equipment. Welker Engineering was able to outsource much of the other machine work because the oil patch was really slow at that time. The company was growing and outgrew its latest building in just a couple of years.

While Bob was involved and engaged in the development of Welker Engineering, Shirley was focused on her love for horses. While they were living in Bellaire, Shirley owned a horse but had to rent space in a barn near their home. The loving husband he had proved to be, Bob was concerned about the clientele that was in and around that barn. When the company was able to purchase 13 acres in Sugar Land, Bob had a horse barn built for Shirley's horses and for renting stalls to other horse people. Shirley ran the Welker Riding Stables. But the first building on that property was a machine shop for Welker Engineering. After twice-a-day trips from Bellaire to Sugar Land, Bob and Shirley built a house on the land and moved into it.

When the company relocated to Sugar Land, Welker Engineering had about half a dozen devices it could sell and 15 or so employees. By that time, Bob had probably 40 patents. He was constantly thinking about ways to improve the devices necessary in his industry. For example, Texsteam had a pump that was very popular in oil fields. However, the pump had a problem with the inlet check valve. Bob considered devising a pump that did not have an inlet check valve. He invented that pump and got a patent on it. Every time you come up with something that will improve your invention, you can get a patent on it, especially if you are the original inventor.

Bob's son, Brian, got his degree in engineering from the University of Houston and went to work for the company. Welker Engineering was growing since it was so relevant to the needs of the petroleum industry. By that time, Bob and Shirley had purchased land in Old Washington, Texas, planning to locate there someday. Since Shirley was still very involved with horses, the first building on that Old Washington land was a horse barn. It was not your typical horse barn. It was nice—for people and for horses. It was clean. It had a bedroom, a bath, and a kitchen. Bob and Shirley lived in it when they went to the ranch. They had agreed with Brian to give him their house in Sugar Land when they relocated to the Old Washington ranch. They weren't in any hurry to move but had it in their plans. One day, Bob heard his young grandson Daniel when he was just a little boy say, "When are they going to move out of our house?" That remark hastened Bob and Shirley's move to Old Washington.

Bob continued his passion at Welker Engineering, driving from Old Washington to Sugar Land daily. With Brian taking responsibility for more and more of the day-to-day operations, Bob was able to cut back some on his hands-on involvement.

Bob and Shirley eventually built a house on the property they called Star Ranch. Together, they combined some small farms into a beautiful estate. In addition to the initial horse barn that they lived in while the house was being built, they built two other barns. One of the newer barns also served as Bob's laboratory where he developed and tested new ideas that would serve the industry.

Shirley began having health problems later in life. On August 5, 2012, she succumbed to a stroke that had debilitated her for some weeks. She was a charter member of the Gulf Coast Belle's Equine Association (later called the Gulf Coast Women's Equine Association).

Shirley Welker

Tomelane Gaskamp, who, with Shirley, envisioned and established the Gulf Coast Women's Equine Association, wrote, "It is with great sadness that I inform you that our organization has lost another valuable and loyal member of 40 years. Shirley Welker died August 5, 2012, in the loving care of her husband, Bob, and other family members, at their Welker Star Ranch in Washington, Texas."

Tomelane continued:

During my years of teaching riding I came to realize the need for a "club" for horse-loving women and their horses to spend time with other horse-loving women and their horses. My Daddy always told me: "There are only two kinds of people in the world—those who love horses and those who don't." I drew on this and approached my friend, Shirley, and told her my idea. She agreed with me and was my right-hand listener and encourager during the planning and organizational phases that resulted in the Gulf Coast Belle's Equine Assn., which is now GCWEA.

Our very first Organizational Meeting in March 1972, was held at Shirley's horse barn. She also, over the years, graciously volunteered to host many other monthly meetings, clinics, committee discussions and planning sessions, trail rides and parties at her Welker Riding Stable business near Sugar Land. The club also enjoyed several family trail rides on Shirley and Bob Welker's ranch near Brenham.

Shirley was elected Vice-President in 1972 and subsequently served in many capacities over the years, including the office of President more

Shirley

Shirley and Tomelane Gaskamp

than once. She was active in GCWEA for 25-plus years, then continued to be a member and in touch by attending the annual Christmas Parties and meetings, the club gatherings for horse shows "at the Dome" during the Houston Live Stock Show, and other occasional clinics and/or social activities.

Our friend, Shirley, loved her horses! She bred, raised, trained and showed both American Quarter Horses and Paints. In her role of stable owner, by daily example, she helped countless women and children to properly feed, groom and exercise their horse. She was a true horse lady, always helpful and supportive in any horse matter. Shirley was a dedicated friend to GCWEA and all its members.

A dear friend to me and my children and my horses for over 45 years, Shirley and I enjoyed our horses in work and in play, "horsing around" together! She and I always knew God had planned our friendship. He even had our daughters introduce us one evening! How awesome is that? Thus, began this friendship that lasted the rest of our lives—for which I shall always be thankful.

Shirley will be greatly missed by many.

After Shirley's memorial service, Bob wrote to Brian and Mindee from his grieving heart:

Some time back, one of our preachers made the statement that an English Queen, on her deathbed, said that she would give everything she owned if she could just live one more hour.

I think of that now because your mother and I never talked about death. Now that she is gone, I think that I would gladly give everything I own to have just two more minutes with her to let her know...

How I have always loved her
How I will always love her
What a great companion she was
What a good mother she was
How helpful she was.

When we started the Welker business she never once complained or failed to meet every challenge that we faced with a cheerful attitude.

I thank God continually for letting me have this wonderful girl for 62 years. Life with your mother was great fun.

The Welker Name

On one of his trips back from the International School of Hydrocarbon Measurement (held annually at the University of Oklahoma), Bob was drowsy. Years of travel had taught him that a remedy to sleepiness was thinking. He began thinking about how weather affected the charts that were so essential to accurate measurement of gas.

The charts recorded the volume and quality of whatever substance was traveling through the pipeline. The information recorded on those charts was absolutely essential to the business running the pipeline. Without accurate measurement, there was no way to determine the amount of substance that was flowing. How could costs and pricing be determined without accurate charts? The work was much too important to leave to guesswork.

Charts had to be read at the same time each period (day, week, month).

The charts were recorded on a disc of high-quality paper. The disc was 12 inches or so in diameter. There was a hole in the center of the disc that allowed the chart to be positioned on a spindle. Automation had found a way to change the chart, but humidity and other weather factors would have a destructive effect on the paper that recorded the vital information. When the device that automatically changed the chart disc knifed in to dislodge the old chart so a new one could resume work, the old chart (affected by weather) would be cut off, resulting in an inaccurate reading.

There had to be some way to improve that necessary process. By the time Bob got to Houston from Norman, Oklahoma, he had it all figured out.

He got a patent on the Welker Dog and sold it for some $600,000. To see what he developed makes one wonder why it hadn't been thought of before. The challenge is always there. Just because it has "always been done that way" doesn't mean "that way" is the best way.

The International School of Hydrocarbon Measurement that Bob regularly attended began in 1924 as Southwestern Gas Measurement Short Course. It is the oldest petroleum industry school in the free world dedicated to fluid measurement and control. W. H. Crutcher, chairman of the Oklahoma Utilities Association, started the first school. Sixty people attended that first school, hosted by the University of Oklahoma. In 1926, Dr. William H. Carson set up the committee structure that serves to this day. Dr. Carson was Dean of the College of Engineering in 1937 and served as head of the Southwestern Gas Measurement Short Course in 1968. In 1972, the Short Course was renamed the International School of Hydrocarbon Measurement and expanded its emphasis to include liquid natural gas and tar sand slurries. One of the pioneers of the school was Laurance Reid. An award named after Reid is awarded annually to a person who has made significant contributions to the industry.

Bob Welker received the Laurance Reid Award in 1993.

On October 26 and 27, 2018, Bob Welker received double honors from his alma mater. On October 26, Bob was inducted into the Engineering Hall of Fame at Texas A&M at Kingsville. When Bob graduated from the university in 1950, it was known as Texas A&I. On October 27, Bob was honored and recognized as Distinguished Alumni.

Brian now serves as chairman and CEO of Welker Inc. The company's catalog states, "With 72 patents under its name, 'Welker' has established itself as an industrious business, successfully improving traditional designs and continually engineering new ones. On average, 'Welker' obtains 3-5 patents on new equipment each year."

Welker Inc. has 18 representatives across the United States and more in 47 countries around the world. While the majority of Welker customers are in the oil and gas industry, products have been and are being engineered for environmental and medical fields.

The Welker Jet (improved from the Jet Stream) is installed in the United States, Canada, Mexico, the United Kingdom, Taiwan, Australia, Belgium, Poland, New Zealand, Germany, France, Iran, Bahrain, Holland, and Thailand.

Javelina Engineering
Hall of Fame 2018

Presented to

Robert H. (Bob) Welker
Class of 1950

In Recognition of Outstanding
Contributions to the
Engineering Profession
and Service to
Javelina Engineering

Distinguished Alumni Award

Presented to

Robert Welker '50

In honor and recognition of your significant
contributions to society and
the accomplishments that
have brought credit to
Texas A&M University-Kingsville

October 26, 2018

Richard "Rick" Garza '98
President
Javelina Alumni Association

Dr. Steven H. Tallant
President
Texas A&M University-Kingsville

INTERNATIONAL
SCHOOL of
HYDROCARBON
MEASUREMENT

Presented annually at

THE UNIVERSITY OF OKLAHOMA

Address reply to

R. L. Grimes
Oklahoma Natural Gas Company
P.O. Box 871
Tulsa, OK 74102-0871

September 14, 1992

Mr. R. H. Welker
Welker Engineering Company
13839 West Belfort
Sugar Land, TX 77478

Dear Bob,

As a friend, and as Chairman of the 1993 Laurance Reid Award Committee, it is with great pleasure that I officially inform you that you have been selected to receive the Laurance Reid Award from the International School of Hydrocarbon Measurement for 1993.

Your nomination came from a number of individuals who were familiar with your contributions to the science and art of measurement and regulation as they pertain to fluid measurement.

Let me be the first to congratulate you and to say that I am proud to be the one to write you this letter.

The committee invites you and Shirley to be our guests at the 1993 school. This invitation includes both your travel and living expenses during the school. We will need to further advise you of your hotel accommodations, but I will assume that they will be at the Sheraton Hotel, downtown Oklahoma City. Eddie Blanchard, Local Arrangements, will have to advise us further on this matter.

I know that you are familiar with the presentation of this award, but there will be a few changes this year from what we have experienced in the past. As you know, the school will be held at the Myriad Center in Oklahoma City in 1993; thus, we will have minor changes.

At this time I assume we will still have our usual General Chairman's Cocktail reception for the principal speaker, and we would certainly want you and Shirley to plan to attend.

Mr. R. H. Welker   2   September 14, 1992

At your earliest convenience, would you please send me a recent photo and information on yourself to be used for the school proceedings and for your award presentation.

If I may be of assistance to you in any way, please do not hesitate to ask. I am looking forward to seeing you at the next committee meeting or at the school.

Sincerely,

R. L. Grimes, Chairman
1993 Laurance Reid Award Committee

c: Mr. R. L. Overbey
   Mr. P. M. Vickery
   Mr. B. F. Ligon

Bob Welker, when active in his company

The Drive: Motive

For what will it profit a man if he gains the whole world, and loses his own soul?

—Mark 8:36 NKJV

Bob Welker understood early on that his inventive mind was a gift from God. Recall this excerpt from a letter home: "Oh yes, the regulator (a gift from God, I believe, because I never set out to think up a new regulator. It just popped into my head and then we had a chance to make something of it)."

Jesus told in the story in Matthew 25:14–30 that each of us has endowments—talents. God's intention is that we use those talents and appreciate the One who gave them to us. "What do you have that you did not receive" (1 Cor. 4:7 NIV). That is a probing question, and there will be a time of accountability.

Bob did have some significant advantages. He was taught a strong ethic. Both sets of grandparents were hardworking people who illustrated for young Bob grit and creative thinking. Bob went to work as early as he was able to. Mowing lawns, delivering prescriptions, mopping floors, hunting pink bollworms, driving spikes on the railroad, maintaining a pipeline for an entire state—all of them and each of them demonstrated his family's commitment to do well at whatever they had to do.

As Bob grew and matured, the heritage of hard work, a willingness to take a risk, and the flexibility that was evident in his family and extended family did not go unnoticed. For his father Harold's work with the USDA, the family had to move around a lot. Bob's mother showed a readiness to do that, to be open to new places, and to endure the rigors of travel in those times with a young family. Moving as often as they did could have been discouraging. For Bob it was an adventure. New places. New adventures. New experiences. All would serve him well as it later became necessary for him to travel extensively—weeks away from home—to actualize his dreams.

What young Bob was learning from his family was honing the innate talents that God had invested in him at birth. One of those talents that Bob recognized—and exercised—was thinking creatively (out-of-the-box). As just a boy, Bob saw this in his grandfather Charles Durning who developed the co-operative of farmers. He saw it in his father, Harold, who searched out employment that would care for the needs of his family and satisfy his own.

What needs to be done? How can it be done? Those are questions that intrigued Bob.

When Tennessee Gas was building a pipeline in New York State, Bob was responsible for the efficient functioning of the measurement and pressure regulation of that line. With such a heavy responsibility and such a large area to supervise, Bob had to think of any possible ways that would make his time more productive and get the job done more easily. It was out of this creative thinking that inventions were born. Bob's thinking could not accept that how it was being done was the only way it could be done. Challenges at work and his time on the road traveling sparked his thinking.

Each of us has time. Managing that time is a challenge. Bob saw his time as prime time for inventions or development. Time—time alone driving, thinking—was significant in Bob's creative process and in his inventions.

Bob's time was also dedicated to his family. Note those heartfelt letters he wrote to them informing, instructing, admonishing, and guiding. His letters told them and showed them that in those many weeks apart, his family was a constant in his life.

Motive is the emotion or desire that causes a person to act. In the words of Jesus in Mark 8:36, "For what will it profit a man if he gains the whole world, and loses his own soul?" Bob worked—and lived—to maximize the endowments God gave him. Exercising those gifts was his motive.

What did Bob Welker profit? Bob's faithful exercise of God-given gifts has produced a company that continues to meet the challenges of the industry.

The Welker name is honored and respected. The family that grew out of Bob and Shirley's marriage is productive and wholesome. Brian and Denise's children all work in the company Bob founded.

In a March 6, 1966, letter, Bob wrote, "God has given each of us a great deal. What shall we do in return?" On April 30, 1967, in a letter home, he said, "You know, I think often of God's grace in our lives and it causes me to stop and reflect on the fact that it is God who in kindness and mercy has given us to one another for a season. Ecclesiastes 3:11." Again on April 30, 1967, he wrote, "We want to be thankful that we can look forward to that season that has no ending. This is with our Lord Jesus."

"What do you have that you did not receive?" has application for everyone.

Bob Welker invested his time, labor, and innovative mind—professionally and personally—with a firm conviction and appreciation for God. He always knew that his creative thinking was a gift from God—the creator of all things and from whom all blessings flow.

Leo Buscaglia said, "Your talent is God's gift to you. What you do with it is your gift back to God."

Bob put it this way: "You see, what we do with the talents God gives us can reflect glory to Him." On October 26, 2018, Bob was honored by his alma mater, now Texas A&M-Kingsville. It is rare for a person to be honored with two recognitions on the same day. On this Homecoming Day, Bob was inducted into the Engineering Hall of Fame. Later that day, he was honored as a Distinguished Alumni. At the Distinguished Alumni recognition, Bob sat with a classmate he had graduated with in 1950.

In the context of living, what shall we do with the gifts with which we have been endowed?

1, 8, 93

Dear Bro Bob Welker

I think after how you help
me out when I start out in the A/C
Business it was a big help to me &
my family what you did for us. I
was thinking about that this morning
in my prayer time & Bible study and
felt I should tell you in a letter how
much you help me, and I thank God
for your understanding in those days.
May you continue to serve the Lord
Christ, and look to Him for your Help.
I wanted you to know I have not forgotten
what you did for me & my family.
Your kindness will always thought of here

Hope this finds you & Shirley well
and in service for Christ. We are going
to Forestwood Bible Church in Humble
TX
our pastor is Charles Snider he is learning
as we are in serving our Lord. Hope your
family well, and in peace.

Thank you again
Pete & Viola Bower

P.S. We are still in the A/C work and are
doing fine by His help.

Letter from a long-time associate

www.ingramcontent.com/pod-product-compliance
Lightning Source LLC
Chambersburg PA
CBHW060814100426
42813CB00004B/1073